SCALES
in First Position
FOR VIOLIN

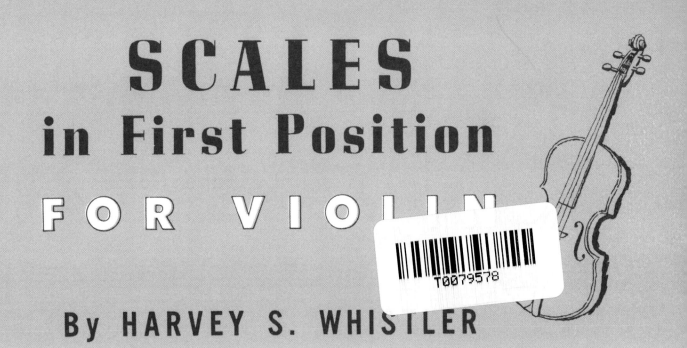

By HARVEY S. WHISTLER

CONTENTS

RUBANK

HAL•LEONARD
CORPORATION
7777 W. BLUEMOUND RD. P.O. BOX 13819 MILWAUKEE, WI 53213

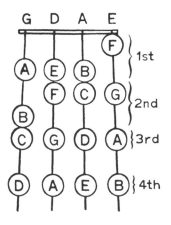

Key of C Major

Détaché Scale

Use détaché bowing in (1) LOWER HALF, (2) MIDDLE, and (3) UPPER HALF of bow.

Slurred Scales

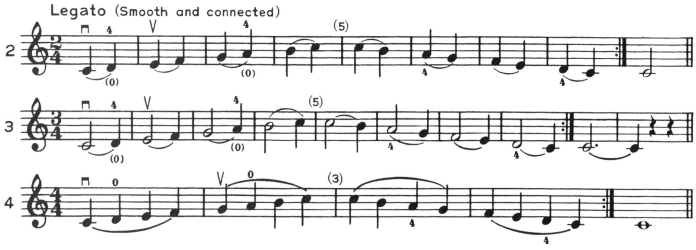

Detached Bowings

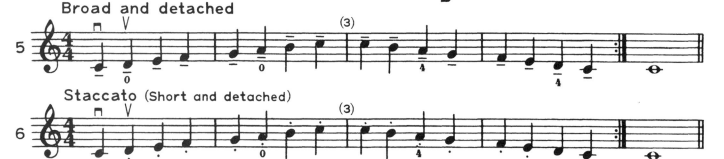

Bow Division

Détaché Scale in Quarter Notes

Use détaché bowing in (1) LOWER HALF, (2) MIDDLE, and (3) UPPER HALF of bow.

Broken Chords

Tone Study

Also practice very slowly, sustaining each tone for EIGHT counts.

Eighth Notes

Also practice (1) slurring each TWO notes, and (2) slurring each FOUR notes.

Quarter and Eighth Notes

Relative Minor Scales

Use détaché bowing in (1) LOWER HALF, (2) MIDDLE, and (3) UPPER HALF of bow.

A Harmonic Minor

17

A Melodic Minor

18

A Minor Chord

19

(1) LH (2) M (3) UH

Minor Scales in Eighth Notes

Also practice (1) slurring each two notes, and (2) slurring each four notes.

A Harmonic Minor

20

A Melodic Minor

21

A Minor Chord in Eighth Notes

22

(1) LH (2) M (3) UH

Major Scales with Staccato Bowing

Use short strokes in (1) LOWER HALF, and (2) MIDDLE of bow.

23

24

Scale and Chord in 6/8 Meter

Triplets

Use (1) LOWER HALF, (2) MIDDLE, and (3) UPPER HALF of bow.

Dotted Eighth and Sixteenth Notes

Use (1) LOWER HALF, (2) MIDDLE, and (3) UPPER HALF of bow. Also practice at the FROG with a separate bow for each note.

Be sure to start UP BOW. Play at extreme tip of stick, using about four inches of hair.

AT POINT

Articulated Scales and Chords

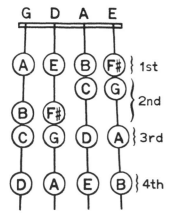

Key of G Major

Détaché Scale

33

Use détaché bowing in (1) LOWER HALF, (2) MIDDLE, and (3) UPPER HALF of bow.

Slurred Scales

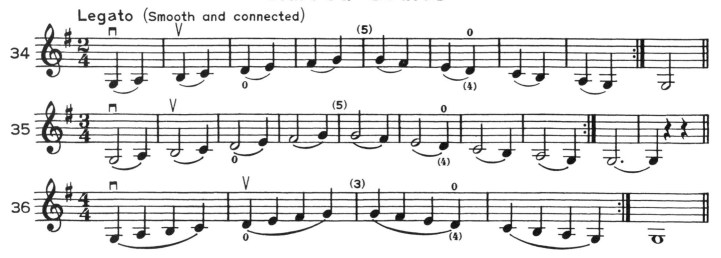

Legato (Smooth and connected)

34

35

36

Detached Bowings

Broad and detached

37

Staccato (Short and detached)

38

Bow Division

39

WB P   WB FR   *simile*

40

WB P   WB FR   *simile*

Détaché Scale in Quarter Notes

41

Use détaché bowing in (1) LOWER HALF, (2) MIDDLE, and (3) UPPER HALF of bow.

Broken Chords

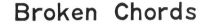

42

43

Tone Study

44

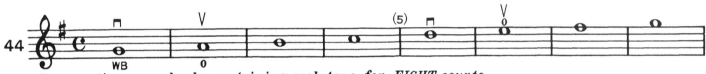

Also practice very slowly, sustaining each tone for EIGHT counts.

Eighth Notes

45

Also practice (1) slurring each TWO notes, and (2) slurring each FOUR notes.

Quarter and Eighth Notes

46

LH M LH FR   *simile*

47

LH M LH FR   *simile*

48

Relative Minor Scales

Use détaché bowing in (1) LOWER HALF, (2) MIDDLE, and (3) UPPER HALF of bow.

E Minor Chord

Minor Scales in Eighth Notes

Also practice (1) slurring each two notes, and (2) slurring each four notes.

E Minor Chord in Eighth Notes

Major Scales with Staccato Bowing

Use short strokes in (1) LOWER HALF, and (2) MIDDLE of bow.

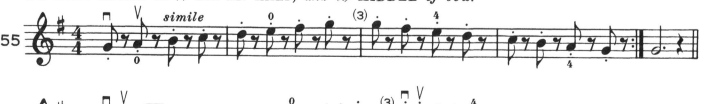

Scale and Chord in 6/8 Meter

57

Triplets

Use (1) LOWER HALF, (2) MIDDLE, and (3) UPPER HALF of bow.

58

Dotted Eighth and Sixteenth Notes

Use (1) LOWER HALF, (2) MIDDLE, and (3) UPPER HALF of bow. Also practice at the FROG with a separate bow for each note.

59

Be sure to start UP BOW. Play at extreme tip of stick, using about four inches of hair.

60

Articulated Scales and Chords

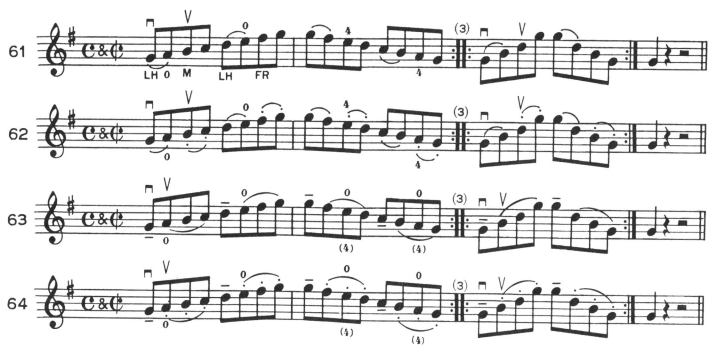

61

62

63

64

9

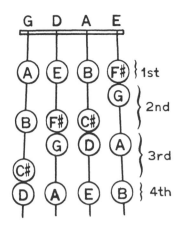

Key of D Major

Détaché Scale

65

Use détaché bowing in (1) LOWER HALF, (2) MIDDLE, and (3) UPPER HALF of bow.

Slurred Scales

Legato (Smooth and connected)

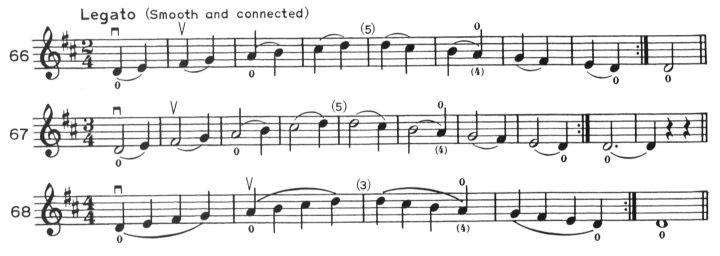

66

67

68

Detached Bowings

Broad and detached

69

Staccato (Short and detached)

70

Bow Division

71

WB   P   WB   FR   *simile*

72

WB   P   WB   FR   *simile*

Détaché Scale in Quarter Notes

73 Use détaché bowing in (1) LOWER HALF, (2) MIDDLE, and (3) UPPER HALF of bow.

Broken Chords

74

75

Tone Study

76 Also practice very slowly, sustaining each tone for EIGHT counts.

Eighth Notes

77 Also practice (1) slurring each TWO notes, and (2) slurring each FOUR notes.

Quarter and Eighth Notes

78

79

80

Relative Minor Scales

Use détaché bowing in (1) LOWER HALF, (2) MIDDLE, and (3) UPPER HALF of bow.

B Minor Chord

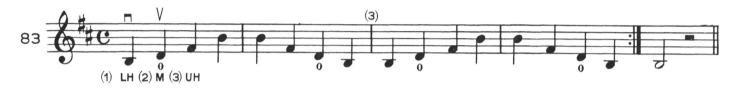

Minor Scales in Eighth Notes

Also practice (1) slurring each two notes, and (2) slurring each four notes.

B Minor Chord in Eighth Notes

Major Scales with Staccato Bowing

Use short strokes in (1) LOWER HALF, and (2) MIDDLE of bow.

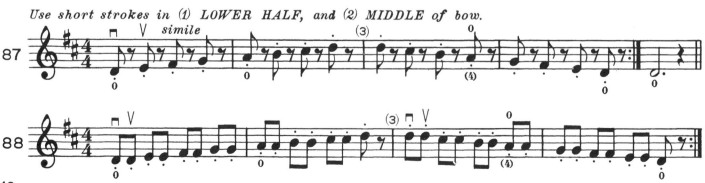

Scale and Chord in 6/8 Meter

Triplets

Use (1) LOWER HALF, (2) MIDDLE, and (3) UPPER HALF of bow.

Dotted Eighth and Sixteenth Notes

Use (1) LOWER HALF, (2) MIDDLE, and (3) UPPER HALF of bow. Also practice at the FROG with a separate bow for each note.

Be sure to start UP BOW. Play at extreme tip of stick, using about four inches of hair.

AT POINT

Articulated Scales and Chords

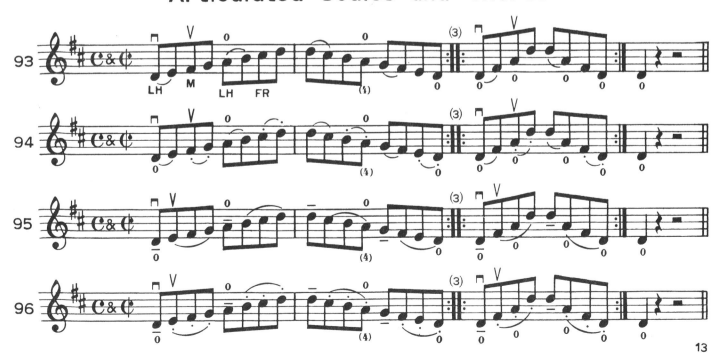

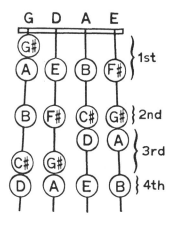

Key of A Major

Détaché Scale

Use détaché bowing in (1) LOWER HALF, (2) MIDDLE, and (3) UPPER HALF of bow.

Slurred Scales

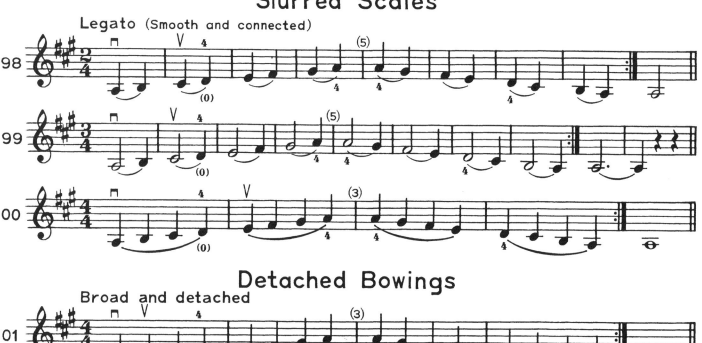

Legato (Smooth and connected)

Detached Bowings

Broad and detached

Staccato (Short and detached)

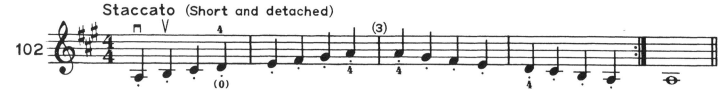

Bow Division

Détaché Scale in Quarter Notes

105 Use détaché bowing in (1) LOWER HALF, (2) MIDDLE, and (3) UPPER HALF of bow.

Broken Chords

106 (1) LH (2) M (3) UH

107 WB

Tone Study

108 WB

Also practice very slowly, sustaining each tone for EIGHT counts.

Eighth Notes

109 Also practice (1) slurring each TWO notes, and (2) slurring each FOUR notes.

Quarter and Eighth Notes

110 LH M LH FR simile

111 LH M LH FR simile

112

15

Relative Minor Scales

Use détaché bowing in (1) LOWER HALF, (2) MIDDLE, and (3) UPPER HALF of bow.

F# Minor Chord

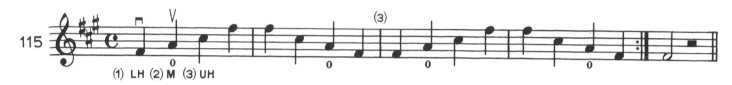

Minor Scales in Eighth Notes

Also practice (1) slurring each two notes, and (2) slurring each four notes.

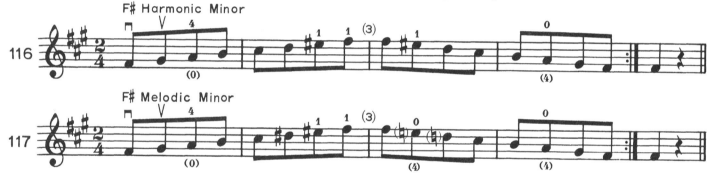

F# Minor Chord in Eighth Notes

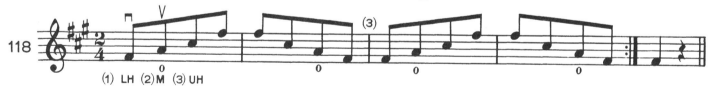

Major Scales with Staccato Bowing

Use short strokes in (1) LOWER HALF, and (2) MIDDLE of bow.

Scale and Chord in 6/8 Meter

121

Triplets

Use (1) LOWER HALF, (2) MIDDLE, and (3) UPPER HALF of bow.

122

Dotted Eighth and Sixteenth Notes

Use (1) LOWER HALF, (2) MIDDLE, and (3) UPPER HALF of bow. Also practice at the FROG with a separate bow for each note.

123

Be sure to start UP BOW. Play at extreme tip of stick, using about four inches of hair.

124

AT POINT

Articulated Scales and Chords

125

126

127

128

Key of F Major

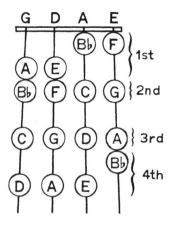

Détaché Scale

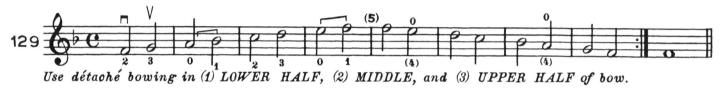

Use détaché bowing in (1) LOWER HALF, (2) MIDDLE, and (3) UPPER HALF of bow.

Slurred Scales

Legato (Smooth and connected)

Detached Bowings

Broad and detached

Staccato (Short and detached)

Bow Division

Détaché Scale in Quarter Notes

137

Use détaché bowing in (1) LOWER HALF, (2) MIDDLE, and (3) UPPER HALF of bow.

Broken Chords

138

(1)LH (2)M (3)UH

139

WB

Tone Study

140

WB

Also practice very slowly, sustaining each tone for EIGHT counts.

Eighth Notes

141

Also practice (1) slurring each TWO notes, and (2) slurring each FOUR notes.

Quarter and Eighth Notes

142

LH M LH FR *simile*

143

LH M LH FR *simile*

144

Relative Minor Scales

Use détaché bowing in (1) LOWER HALF, (2) MIDDLE, and (3) UPPER HALF of bow.

D Harmonic Minor

145

D Melodic Minor

146

D Minor Chord

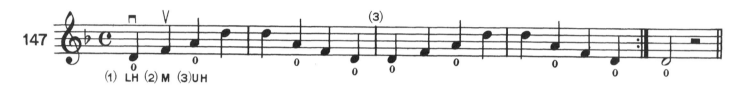

147

(1) LH (2) M (3) UH

Minor Scales in Eighth Notes

Also practice (1) slurring each two notes, and (2) slurring each four notes.

D Harmonic Minor

148

D Melodic Minor

149

D Minor Chord in Eighth Notes

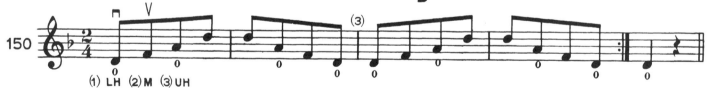

150

(1) LH (2) M (3) UH

Major Scales with Staccato Bowing

Use short strokes in (1) LOWER HALF, and (2) MIDDLE of bow.

simile

151

152

Scale and Chord in 6/8 Meter

153

Triplets

Use (1) LOWER HALF, (2) MIDDLE, and (3) UPPER HALF of bow.

154

Dotted Eighth and Sixteenth Notes

Use (1) LOWER HALF, (2) MIDDLE, and (3) UPPER HALF of bow. Also practice at the FROG with a separate bow for each note.

155

Be sure to start UP BOW. Play at extreme tip of stick, using about four inches of hair.

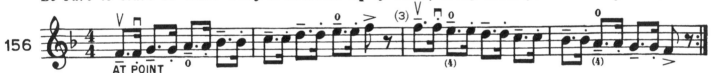

156

Articulated Scales and Chords

157

158

159

160

Key of B♭ Major

Détaché Scale

161 *Use détaché bowing in (1) LOWER HALF, (2) MIDDLE, and (3) UPPER HALF of bow.*

Slurred Scales

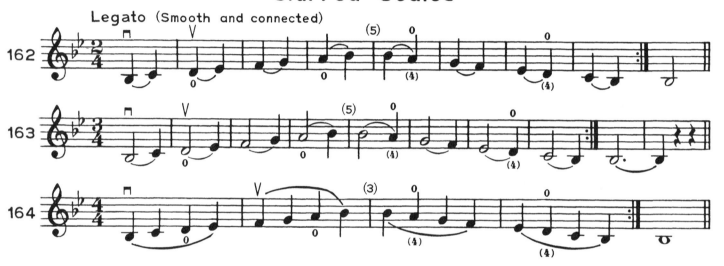

Legato (Smooth and connected)

162

163

164

Detached Bowings

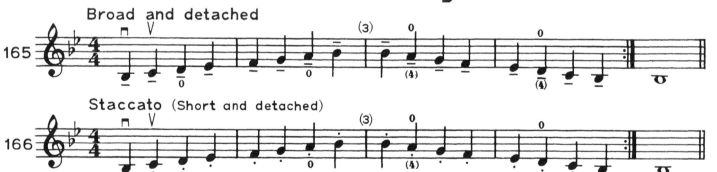

Broad and detached

165

Staccato (Short and detached)

166

Bow Division

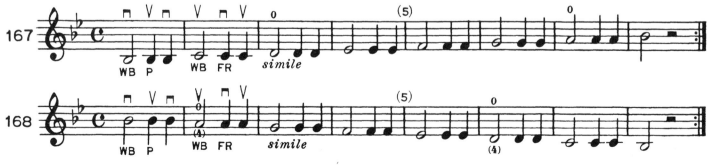

167

168

Détaché Scale in Quarter Notes

169

Use détaché bowing in (1) LOWER HALF, (2) MIDDLE, and (3) UPPER HALF of bow.

Broken Chords

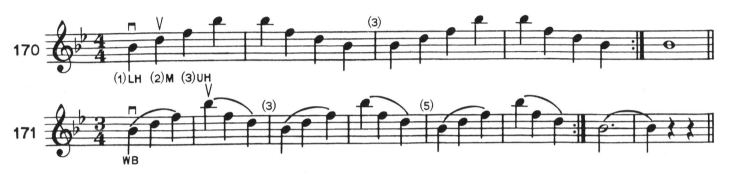

170

171

WB

Tone Study

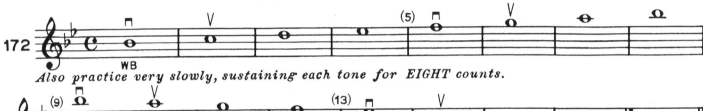

172

WB

Also practice very slowly, sustaining each tone for EIGHT counts.

Eighth Notes

173

Also practice (1) slurring each TWO notes, and (2) slurring each FOUR notes.

Quarter and Eighth Notes

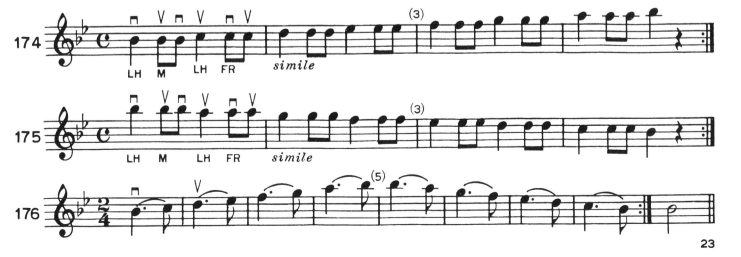

174

LH   M   LH   FR   *simile*

175

LH   M   LH   FR   *simile*

176

Relative Minor Scales

Use détaché bowing in (1) LOWER HALF, (2) MIDDLE, and (3) UPPER HALF of bow.

G Minor Chord

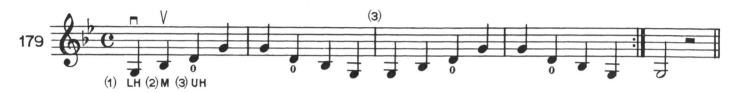

Minor Scales in Eighth Notes

Also practice (1) slurring each two notes, and (2) slurring each four notes.

G Minor Chord in Eighth Notes

Major Scales with Staccato Bowing

Use short strokes in (1) LOWER HALF, and (2) MIDDLE of bow.

Scale and Chord in 6/8 Meter

185

Triplets

Use (1) LOWER HALF, (2) MIDDLE, and (3) UPPER HALF of bow.

186

Dotted Eighth and Sixteenth Notes

Use (1) LOWER HALF, (2) MIDDLE, and (3) UPPER HALF of bow. Also practice at the FROG with a separate bow for each note.

187

Be sure to start UP BOW. Play at extreme tip of stick, using about four inches of hair.

188

AT POINT

Articulated Scales and Chords

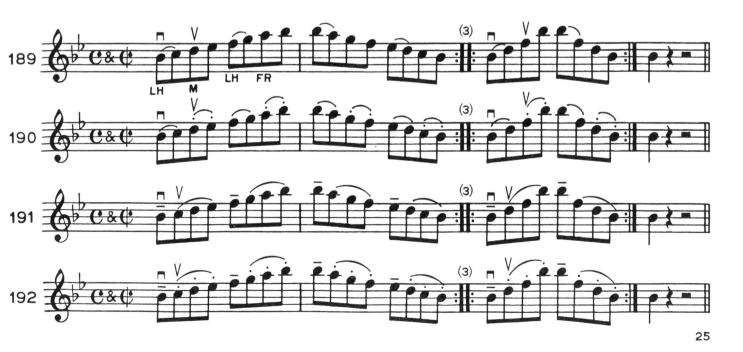

189

190

191

192

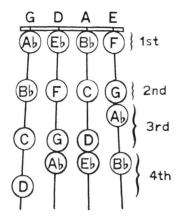

Key of E♭ Major

Détaché Scale

193

Use détaché bowing in (1) LOWER HALF, (2) MIDDLE, and (3) UPPER HALF of bow.

Slurred Scales

Legato (Smooth and connected)

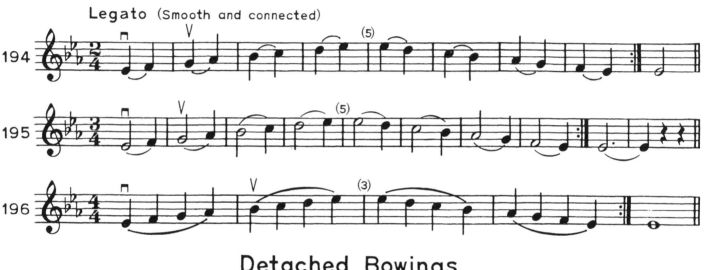

194

195

196

Detached Bowings

Broad and detached

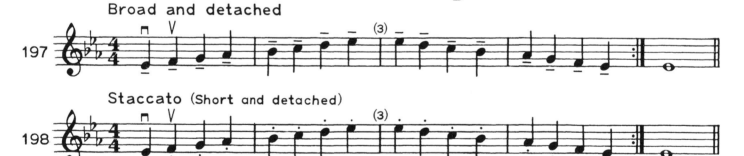

197

Staccato (Short and detached)

198

Bow Division

199

WB   P   WB FR   *simile*

200

WB   P   WB FR   *simile*

Détaché Scale in Quarter Notes

201

Use détaché bowing in (1) LOWER HALF, (2) MIDDLE, and (3) UPPER HALF of bow.

Broken Chords

202

(1)LH (2)M (3)UH

203

WB

Tone Study

204

WB

Also practice very slowly, sustaining each tone for EIGHT counts.

205

Eighth Notes

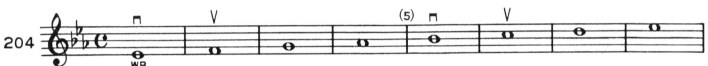

205

Also practice (1) slurring each TWO notes, and (2) slurring each FOUR notes.

Quarter and Eighth Notes

206

LH M LH FR *simile*

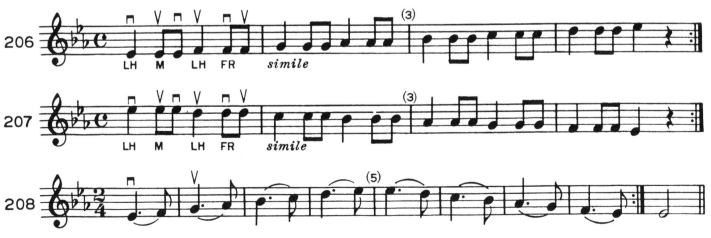

207

LH M LH FR *simile*

208

Relative Minor Scales

Use détaché bowing in (1) LOWER HALF, (2) MIDDLE, and (3) UPPER HALF of bow.

C Minor Chord

Minor Scales in Eighth Notes

Also practice (1) slurring each two notes, and (2) slurring each four notes.

C Minor Chord in Eighth Notes

Major Scales with Staccato Bowing

Use short strokes in (1) LOWER HALF, and (2) MIDDLE of bow.

Scale and Chord in 6/8 Meter

Triplets

Use (1) LOWER HALF, (2) MIDDLE, and (3) UPPER HALF of bow.

Dotted Eighth and Sixteenth Notes

Use (1) LOWER HALF, (2) MIDDLE, and (3) UPPER HALF of bow. Also practice at the FROG with a separate bow for each note.

Be sure to start UP BOW. Play at extreme tip of stick, using about four inches of hair.

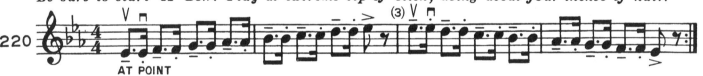

AT POINT

Articulated Scales and Chords

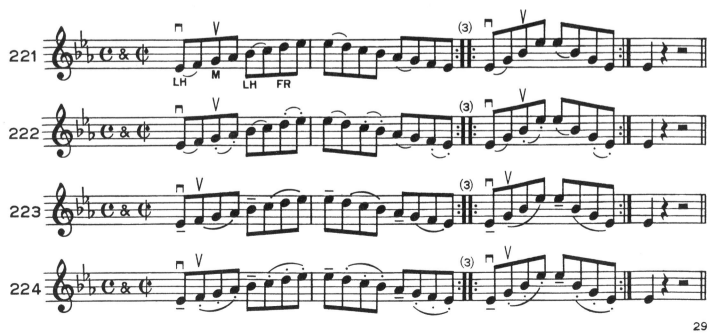

LH   M   LH   FR

Daily Scale Exercises

Draw bow slowly.
Keep each finger down as long as possible.
Also practice (1) using a separate bow for each note, and (2) slurring each two measures.

Scales in Broken Thirds

Also practice (1) using a separate bow for each note, and (2) slurring each complete measure.

Scale in Broken Sixths

Chromatic Scales

Also practice (1) slurring each TWO notes, and (2) slurring each FOUR notes.

245

246

247

248

249

250

251

Extended Chromatic Scale

252

Also practice (1) slurring each TWO notes, and (2) slurring each FOUR notes.